Dear Mary Catherine

So sorry we are having so much rain

Have a Happy Birthday

All Our Love

Bob & Mary

Happy birthday

A Treasury of Joyful Thought and Beautiful Verse on your Special Day

Susan Power

Designed by
Philip Clucas

Produced by
Ted Smart and David Gibbon

MAYFLOWER BOOKS · NEW YORK CITY

A year is...

A year is...
　a lane overhung with Winter snowflakes,
　a meadow where early Spring has been,
　sparkling dew that clings to a Summer's rose,
　Autumn's gold-coinage of falling sunlight.

A year is...
　three hundred and sixty-five
　days of beauty...
　three hundred and sixty-five reasons for joy.

A birthday is like the gift of morning sunlight
　to the spirit. It reawakens the miracle
　of being, and makes us suddenly aware
　of the beauty that surrounds us.
It is to be filled as never before with the
　daily wonder of living in a world that
　shines with hope.
A birthday is a day of inspiration, to brighten
　all your days: a day to cherish
　and to share with those you love.

As a new year of your life begins,
now is a time to dream –
to look forward with excitement to
a future filled with possibilities –
for those who do not dream
have never known the delight of
a wish come true.

All the wars of the world,
     all the Cæsars,
have not the staying power
     of a lily in a cottage border . . .
The immortality of marble
     and of miseries
          is a vain, small thing
compared to the immortality
     of a flower that blooms
          and is dead by dusk.

Today is your birthday.
It is a day to know, and feel, the wide world.
It is a day of budding leaf, of opening flower,
     and silent greenness.
It is a day to listen to the rustle of birds'
     wings as they fly unseen in the wood.
It is a day to wonder why thistledown
     is flying though the winds are still.
It is a dawn of silver mist,
     it is a morning of billowing cloud,
          it is an evening of Summer-fire set in the west.

     It is a day to celebrate –
          a day of many hidden blessings.

Day! Faster and more fast,
over night's brim, day boils at last;
… forth one wavelet, then another, curled,
'til the whole sunrise, not to be suppressed,
rose … reddened, and its seething breast
flickered in bounds, grew gold,
then overflowed the world.

Today is Your Day

Today is Your Day –
a day to think of all
    the places that you have visited –
    a day to think of all
    the people that you have known.

    Today is Your Day –
    a day to consider all
the big, and all the little events
    that, over the years, have made
    your life unique.
Today, fill your heart with their
    pride and with their pleasure.

The Gardener

I bought flowering trees
and planted them out on the eastern bank.
I simply bought whatever had most blooms,
not caring whether peach, apricot or plum.
A hundred fruits, all mixed up together;
a thousand branches, flowering in due rotation.
Each has its season, coming early or late;
but to all alike the fertile soil is kind.
The red flowers hang like a heavy mist;
the white flowers gleam like a snow-fall.
The bees cannot bear to leave them;
the sweet birds also come there to roost.
In front there flows an ever-running stream;
beneath there is built a little flat terrace.
Sometimes I sweep the flagstones of the terrace;
sometimes, in the wind, I raise my cup and drink.
The flower-branches screen my head from the sun;
the flower-buds fall down into my lap.
Alone singing my song,
I do not notice that the moon is risen.

Po-Chü-I

Nature is painting for us,
day after day, pictures of
infinite beauty if only
we have the eyes to see them.

JOHN RUSKIN

Butterflies

As butterflies are but winged flowers.
　　　half sorry for their change, who fain,
so still and long they live on leaves,
　　　would be thought flowers again –
E'en so my thoughts, that should expand,
　　　and grow to higher themes above,
return like butterflies to lie
　　　on the old things I love.

The sunshine of life
　　is made up of small beams
　　　that are bright all the time.

Dewdrops in Spring

The dewdrops on every blade of grass are so
much like silver drops that I am obliged to stoop
down as I walk to see if they are pearls, and those
sprinkled on the ivy-woven beds of primroses
underneath the hazels, whitethorns and maples are so
like gold beads that I stooped down to feel if they were
hard, but they melted from my finger. And where the
dew lies on the primrose, the violet and whitethorn
leaves, they are emerald and beryl, yet nothing more
than the dews of the morning on the budding leaves;
nay, the field grasses are covered with gold and silver
beads, and the further we go the brighter they seem to
shine, like solid gold and silver. It is nothing more than
the sun's light and shade upon them in the dewy
morning; every thorn-point and every bramble-spear
has its trembling ornament: until the wind gets a little
brisker, and then all is shaken off, and all the shining
jewelry passes away into a common Spring morning
full of budding leaves, primroses, violets, vernal
speedwell, bluebell and orchids, and commonplace
objects.

JOHN CLARE

To accomplish great things,
we must not only act but also dream,
not only plan but also believe.

ANATOL FRANCE

Loveliest of trees, the cherry now
    is hung with bloom along the bough,
and stands about the woodland ride
    wearing white for Eastertide.

Now of my threescore years and ten,
    twenty will not come again,
and take from seventy Springs a score,
    it only leaves me fifty more.

And since to look at things in bloom
    fifty Springs are little room,
about the woodlands I will go
    to see the cherry hung with snow.

A. E. HOUSEMAN

It's your day,
so here's wishing you
happiness, peace of mind,
sunny skies, and, most of all . . .
the deep joy of knowing
that you are exactly who you are!

Although we travel the world over to find beauty,
we must carry it with us or we will find it not.

First published in 1980 by Colour Library International Ltd.
© 1980 Illustrations and text: Colour Library International Ltd.,
163 East 64th St., New York, N.Y. 10021.
Colour separations by FERCROM, Barcelona, Spain.
Display and text filmsetting by Focus Photoset, London, England.
Printed and bound by JISA-RIEUSSET, Barcelona, Spain.
All rights reserved. ISBN 8317-0891-3
**Published in the United States of America
by Mayflower Books, Inc., New York City.**